THE WORLD OF HENRI CARTIER BRESSON

BY HENRI CARTIER-BRESSON

A STUDIO BOOK · THE VIKING PRESS · NEW YORK

The major part of the text in this book is a reworking of the ideas I set down sixteen years ago in my first book, *Images à la Sauvette.* Basically my ideas have not changed since then. The book was published in English as *The Decisive Moment,* for which my thanks are still due to *Verve* and to Simon and Schuster. I am also most grateful to Robert Delpire for his valuable help in preparing this book.

PREFACE

In my view photography has not changed since its origins, except in technical aspects, and these are not my major preoccupation. Photography is an instantaneous operation, both sensory and intellectual—an expression of the world in visual terms, and also a perpetual quest and interrogation. It is at one and the same time the recognition of a fact in a fraction of a second and the rigorous arrangement of the forms visually perceived which give to that fact expression and significance.

The chief requirement is to be fully involved in this reality which we delineate in the viewfinder. The camera is to some extent a sort of notebook for recording sketches made in time and space, but it is also an admirable instrument for seizing upon life as it presents itself. Without the participation of intuition, sensibility, and understanding, photography is nothing. All these faculties must be closely harnessed, and it is then that the capture of a rare picture becomes a real physical delight.

Photography appears to be a simple matter, but it demands powers of concentration combined with mental enthusiasm and discipline. It is by strict economy of means that simplicity of expression is achieved. A photographer must always work with the greatest respect for his subject and in terms of his own point of view. That is my own personal attitude; consequently I have a marked prejudice against "arranged" photographs and contrived settings.

The intensive use of photographs by mass media lays ever fresh responsibilities upon the photographer. We have to acknowledge the existence of a chasm between the economic needs of our consumer society and the requirements of those who bear witness to this epoch. This affects us all, particularly the younger generations of photographers. We must take greater care than ever not to allow ourselves to be separated from the real world and from humanity.

H.C.-B.   February 22, 1968

THE SUBJECT. A subject is not a collection of facts, for facts in themselves offer little interest. The important thing is how to choose between them, how to fix on the fact that bears the stamp of profound reality—how, in short, to place oneself in relation to what one perceives.

In photography the smallest thing may be a challenging subject; some small human detail can become a kind of leitmotif. In what we see and reveal to others we are witnesses of the world around us; and events, by their very nature, instigate the disposition of forms and their rhythm. As regards method of expression, there are so many thousand ways of distilling what appeals to us that this question must remain open.

There is one domain which photography has won away from painting—or so it is claimed—and that is portraiture. Faced with the camera, people proffer their best "profile" to posterity. It is their hope, blended with a certain magic fear, to outlive themselves in this portrait, and here they give us a hold. The first impression we have of a face is frequently correct; if to this first impression others are added by further acquaintance, the better we know the person the harder it becomes to pick out the essential qualities. One of the touching features of portraiture is that it reveals the permanence of mankind, even if only in the family album. We must respect the surroundings which provide the subject's true setting, while avoiding all artifice which destroys the authentic image. The mere presence of the photographer and his camera affects the behavior of the "victim." Massive

apparatus and flash bulbs prevent the subject from being himself.

What is more fugitive than a facial expression? Whether the portrait has been commissioned by the sitter or by some editor, it is always a tricky undertaking. The first client often wants to be flattered; the second absolves you from this obligation and merely leaves you to cope with your own difficulties.

Sometimes it seems as though the model is more fearful of the objectivity of the camera than of the subjectivity and psychological acuity of the photographer. Yet these factors are so predominant that one recognizes an affinity of approach between various portraits by the same photographer. Rather than the artificial style which verges on the pompous and grotesque, give me those rows of little identity snapshots crammed together in the windows of passport photographers. At least they provide a record of a physiognomy, even if they lack that synthesis of a whole personality which one hopes to capture.

COMPOSITION. We must place ourselves and our camera in the right relationship with the subject, and it is in fitting the latter into the frame of the viewfinder that the problems of composition begin. This recognition, in real life, of a rhythm of surfaces, lines, and values is for me the essence of photography; composition should be a constant preoccupation, being a simultaneous coalition—an organic coordination of visual elements. Composition does not just happen; there must be a need for expression, and substance cannot be divorced from form.

Photography, being dependent on reality, raises plastic problems which must be solved by the use of our eyes and by the adjustment of our camera. We keep changing our perspective in continual movement governed by rapid reflexes. We compose almost at the moment of pressing the shutter, moving through minutiae of space and time. Sometimes one remains motionless, waiting for something to happen; sometimes the situation is resolved and there is nothing to photograph. If something should happen, you remain alert, wait a bit, then shoot and go off with the sensation of having got something. Later you can amuse yourself by tracing out on the photo the geometrical pattern, or spatial relationships, realizing that, by releasing the shutter at that precise instant, you had instinctively selected an exact geometrical harmony, and that without this the photographs would have been lifeless. But to apply a golden rule, the photographer's compass can be nowhere but in his eye. Obviously any geometrical analysis or reduction to a set of values can be undertaken only in retrospect, and only as matter for reflection. It is by means of form, by careful plastic organization, that our thoughts and emotions become communicable.

REPORTAGE. Photo-reporting presents the essentials of a problem, or it records an event or impressions. An event is so rich in possibilities that you hover around while it develops. You hunt for the solution. Sometimes you find it in the fraction of a second; sometimes it takes hours, or even days. There is no standard solution, no recipe; you must be alert, as in a game of tennis.

The elements in a situation that touch off the spark are often diffuse; we have no right to bring them together by force, and to stage them would be trickery, hence the use of layout in publications; on the printed page the various complementary elements depicted in a number of photographs are brought together.

Reality offers us such a rich abundance that we have to simplify, to make a selection, but do we always choose rightly? In the course of our work we have to attain a certain discipline, an awareness of what we are about. Sometimes I think I have taken *the* master photo, but I go on shooting because I can never be sure how any event will turn out. We must, however, refrain from snapping rapidly and mechanically, because in this way we only burden ourselves with useless shots that encumber the memory and cloud the clarity of the whole.

The photographer cannot be a passive spectator; he can be really lucid only if he is caught up in the event. Memory is most important—to remember each photograph taken while keeping pace with the event. While on the job he must be sure he has left no gaps, that every facet is expressed, because afterward it will be too late, and he cannot turn back the clock.

We are faced with two moments of selection and thus of possible regret: the first and more serious when actuality is there, staring us in the viewfinder; and the second when all the shots have been developed and printed and we have to reject the less effective ones. It is then—too late—that we see exactly where we have failed. When we are at work, a moment's hesitation or physical separation from the event robs us of some detail; all too often we have let our eye wander, we have lost our concentration; that is enough.

For everyone, space extends outward from the eye to infinity over a scene which strikes us with differing degrees of intensity, only to pass at once into our memory and there be modified. Of all forms of expression, photography is the only one which seizes the instant in its flight. We look for the evanescent, the irreplaceable; this is our constant concern, and therefore one of the characteristics of our craft. We must not retouch; all we can do is choose among the shots that we have, so as to present an intelligible account. A writer has time to let phrases form themselves before he commits them to paper; he can make an interplay of varying elements; whereas we, once we are back home, can do nothing more about our reportage. Our job is to view events with a clinical eye and to record them, but not to distort them by means of tricks, either while shooting or in the dark room.

In this type of photography one comes to count the strokes, rather like an umpire, but one is, alas, always an intruder. Approach the subject on tiptoe, even if it is a still life. Let your steps be velvet but your eye keen; a good fisherman does not stir up the water before he starts to fish. There is no question, of course, of flash photos, even if only out of respect for the light, however evanescent; otherwise the photographer appears intolerably aggressive. Our job is immensely dependent on contacts with people; one false word and they withdraw. Here again, there is no set system, unless it be to pass unnoticed, together with one's camera, which is always conspicuous. Reactions differ enormously between countries and between social groups; anywhere in the East, for example, a photographer who is impatient or merely in a hurry covers himself with ridicule, and this is irremediable. If ever you lose contact and someone notices your camera, you might just as well forget photography and let the children clamber around you.

I have written at length about reportage, because this is what I do. But through it I try, desperately, to achieve the single photograph which exists for its own sake.

TECHNIQUE. The choice of format plays a great part in the expression of the subject. A square format, owing to the equality of its sides, tends to be static (there are, incidentally, very few square paintings). If you crop a good photograph, no matter how slightly, you necessarily destroy the play of proportions. On the other hand, it is seldom indeed that a composition which was poor when the picture was taken can be improved by reshaping it in the dark room. Nibbling away at the negative under the enlarger destroys the visual integrity. Personally, I have never succeeded in making a strong photograph out of a poor one by taking a detail and reframing the picture. In my opinion there must be a totality, an integrity, in the original shot. It is at this moment only, and by taking a new photograph if possible, that a composition can be corrected. There is a lot of talk about "angles of view," but the only angles I acknowledge are those of geometry and composition.

In speaking of aesthetics and technique, I have had in mind the convention of black and white, that symbolic transposition of all living colors. Color photography, in so-called natural colors, adds a host of hazards. Personally I fear that this element, so difficult to control on the printed page, may be detrimental to what, in my view, is its real strength. In order, genuinely, to create in color photography, it is necessary to transpose or change the colors and thus be at liberty to express oneself within the limits of the great laws of painting, from which no one can escape. (In the law of simultaneous contrast, any color tends to impress on the space around it its own complementary color; if two tints have a color in common, this will be weakened by their juxtaposition; two complementary colors juxtaposed enhance each other, but mixed they kill one another—and so on.) But it is certain that color photography depends on the improvements that science and technique will bring.

Chemistry, physics, and optics enlarge our scope; it is for us to apply them as part of our technique in order to see whether they can add to what we wish to express. But a whole fetishism has grown up around the technique of photography. Technique should be so conceived and adapted as to induce a way of seeing things, preferably in essentials, excluding the effects of gratuitous virtuosity and other ineptitudes. Technique is important in that we have to master it, but it is the result that counts. Our profession of reporting has existed for only some thirty years; it has advanced thanks to small and handy cameras, wide-angle lenses, and ultra-rapid fine-grain films. For us the camera is a tool, the extension of our eye, not a pretty little mechanical toy. It is sufficient that we should feel at ease with the camera best adapted for our purpose. Adjustments of the camera—such as setting the aperture and the speed—should become reflexes, like changing gear in a car. The real problem is one of intelligence and sensitivity.

When enlarging the negative we must respect the values of the original shot and, in order to render them faithfully, re-create the atmosphere of the original scene. We must re-establish the balance which our eye constantly makes between light and shadow, and this is why the final phase of photographic creation occurs in the dark room. I am always amused at the notion that some people have about photographic technique, expressed by a mania for the sharpness of the line or a grain exaggeratedly enlarged. Does this spring from a passion for titivation or do they hope by these delusions to get the better of their own insensitivity? They are as far from grasping the true problem as were those photographers of another generation who shrouded themselves in soft-focus effects.

THE USERS. The camera enables us to keep a kind of visual record. We photo-reporters are people who supply information to a world in haste and swamped, willy-nilly, in a morass of printed matter. This abbreviation of the statement which is the language of photography is very potent; we express, in effect, an adjudgment of what we see, and this demands intellectual honesty. We work in terms of reality, not of fiction, and must therefore "discover," not fabricate.

Between the public and ourselves there stands the printed page, which, together with the screen, forms the main channel of circulation for our output; we are artisans who supply the raw material. I was genuinely moved when I sold my first photograph (to *Vu*); it was the beginning of a long alliance with illustrated magazines. It is they who bring out what we are trying to say; unfortunately they sometimes deform it—but that can't be helped. Also, of course, the photographer is in danger of being influenced by the tastes and requirements of the magazines. As for captions, these should be the verbal counterpoint to the pictures, adding what is necessary or establishing them in their context. Here, too, errors occur which are not always due to a slip at the printer's.

The great quality of a good layout man is the ability to select from among the sheaf of photographs submitted to him those which merit a whole page or a double page, and to know how to insert the little shot that forms the link. He sometimes has to crop a picture, keeping only the part that he finds most important, since his chief preoccupation is the harmony of the page; thus the photographer's composition is modified. Yet our thanks are due to the layout man for a good presentation, where the photographs are framed in proper margins and where the design of each page, and the rhythm and balance of the whole, present the story as we conceived it.

The photographer's final anxiety comes when he leafs through the magazine, sees the story as a whole, and discovers how his vision of things has been interpreted.

I have written at some length about one aspect of photography, but there are many others, ranging from the photographs in a sales catalogue or fashion magazine to the touching snapshots turning yellow in the back of a wallet. Decidedly I have set out here to give a definition not of photography but only of the kind that I try to achieve.

NOTE

The pictures in the six sections that follow are not intended to give a general idea of any particular country, but I am quite unable to assert that the subjects depicted are imaginary and that any resemblance to any individual is coincidental.

1

1

2

4

6

7

9

15

20

21

22

23

24

25

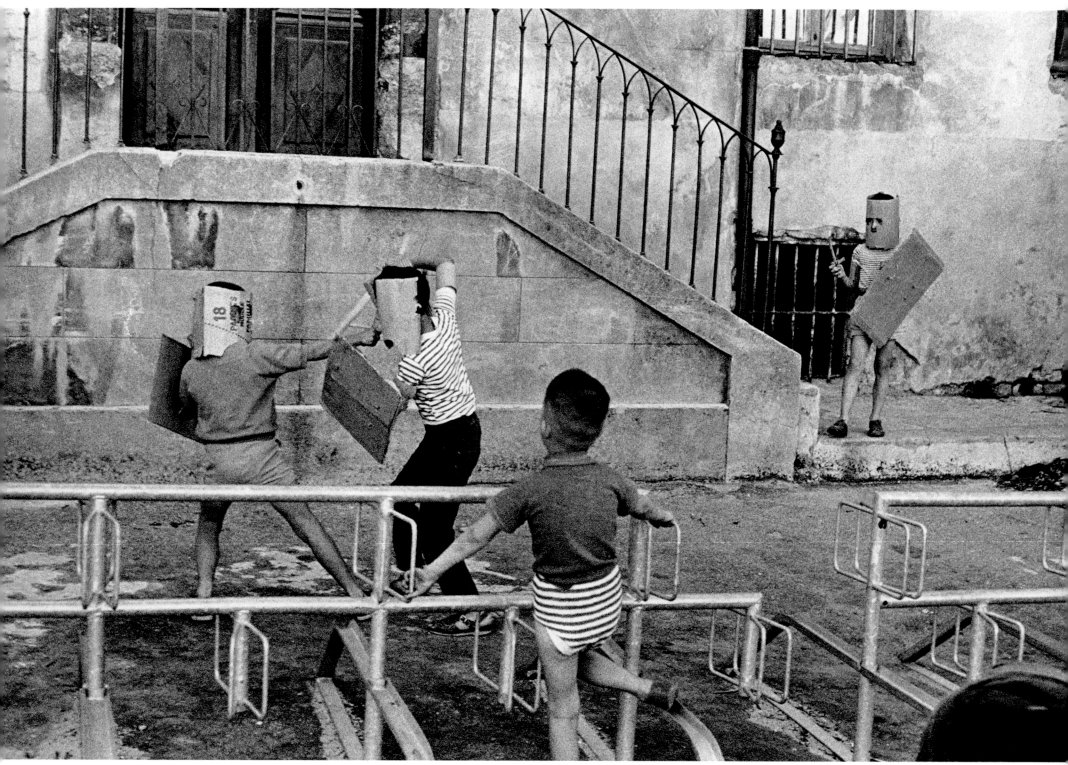

35

38

39

43

44

45

46

59

61

3

65

66

68

69

71

74

75

76

77

80

83

84

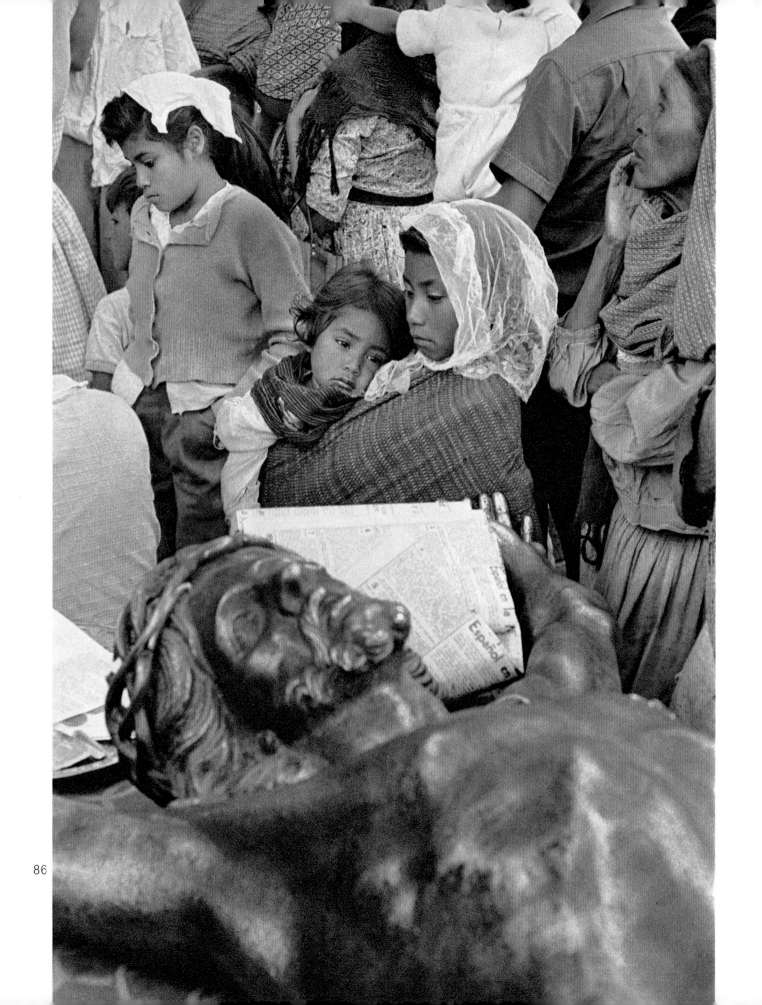

93

96

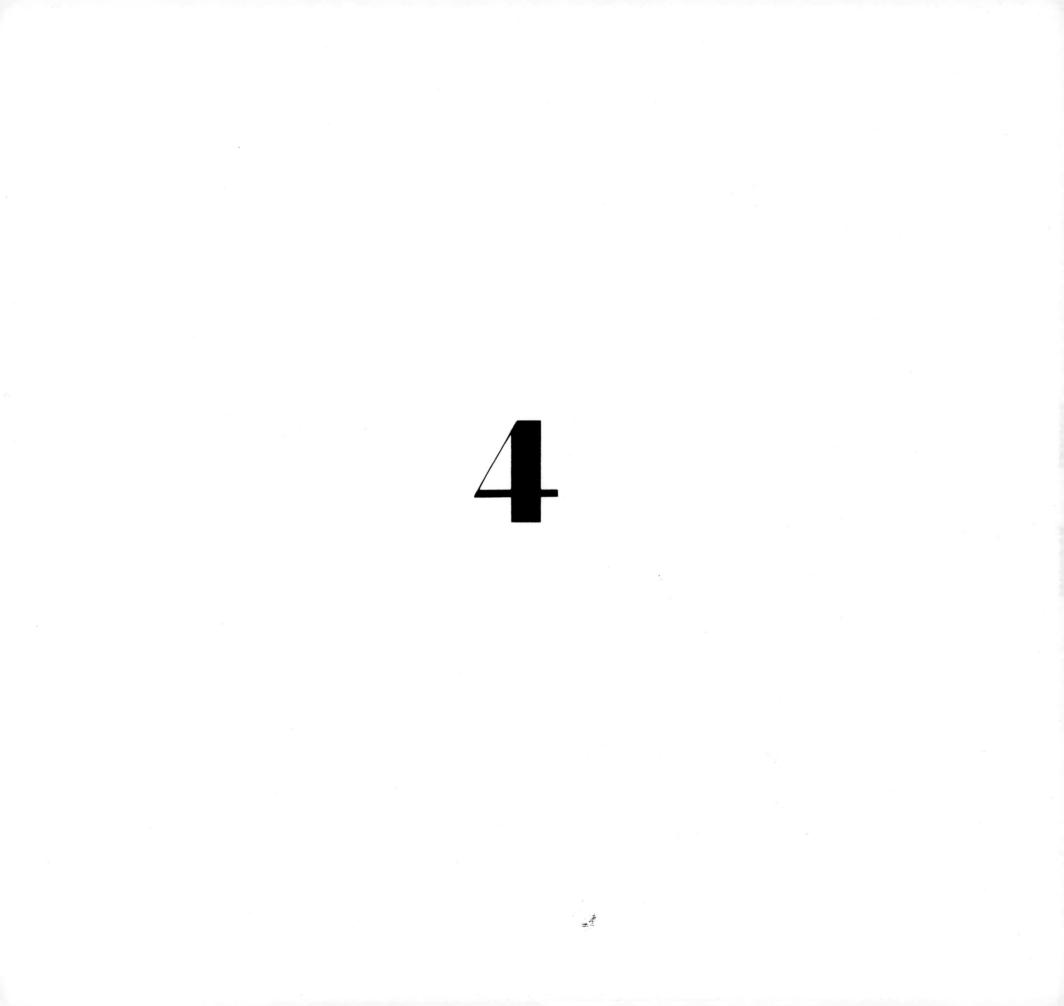

110

111

119

131

134

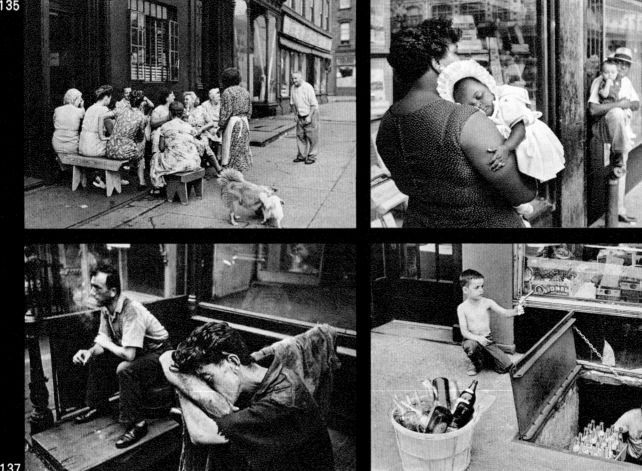

141

142

143

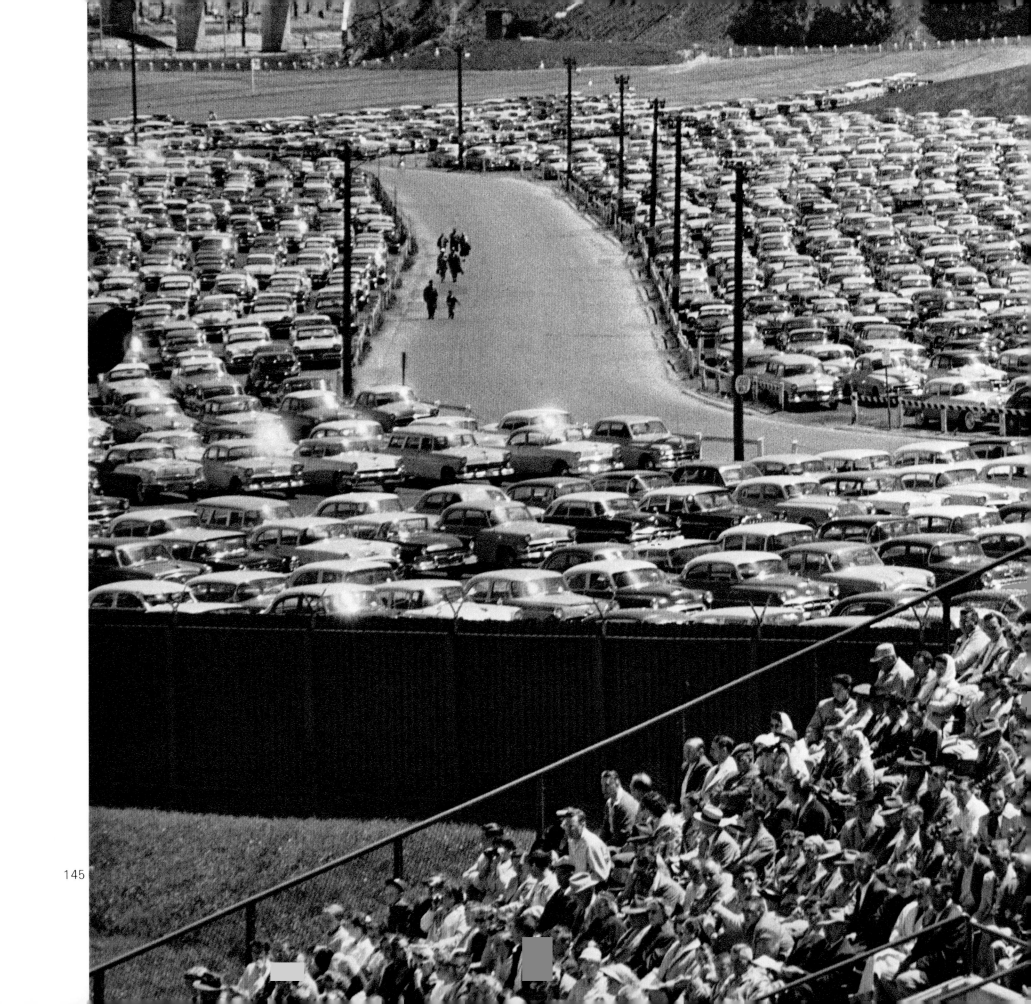

152

153

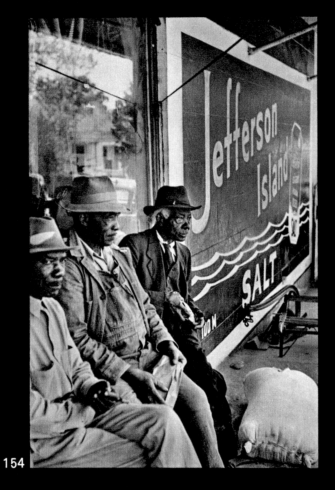

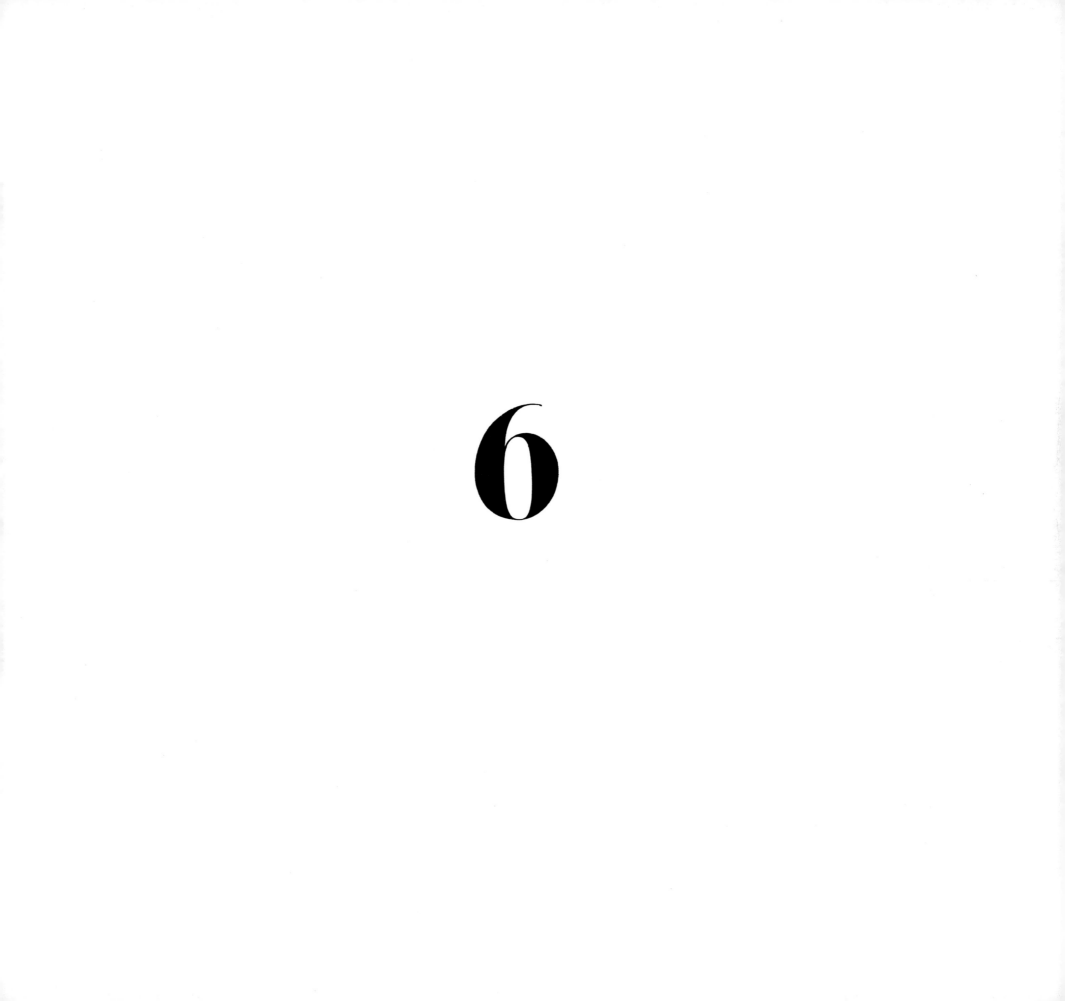

6

159

163

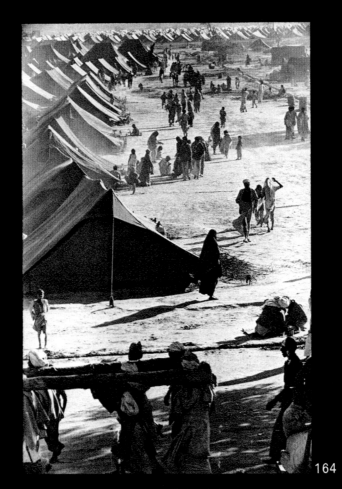

164

170

184

187

194

195

197

207

208

CAPTIONS